cloverleaf books™

My Healthy Habits

Choose Good Food!

My Eating Tips

Gina Bellisario

illustrated by Holli Conger

M MILLBROOK PRESS • MINNEAPOLIS

For Paul, our healthy chef —G.B.

For my little kitchen helpers, who
make mealtime fun! —H.C.

Millbrook Press
A division of Lerner Publishing Group, Inc.
241 First Avenue North
Minneapolis, MN 55401 USA

For reading levels and more information, look up this title at
www.lernerbooks.com.

Main body text set in Slappy Inline 18/28.
Typeface provided by T26.

Library of Congress Cataloging-in-Publication Data

Bellisario, Gina.
    Choose good food!: My eating tips / by Gina Bellisario ;
illustrated by Holli Conger.
        p.   cm — (Cloverleaf books™—My healthy habits)
    Includes index.
    ISBN 978–1–4677–1350–4 (lib. bdg. : alk. paper)
    ISBN 978–1–4677–2534–7 (eBook)
    1. Nutrition—Juvenile literature. 2. Food habits—Juvenile
literature. 3. Lunchbox cooking—Juvenile literature. I. Conger,
Holli, illustrator. II. Title.
TX355.B458 2014
613.2—dc23   2013014299

Manufactured in the United States of America
1 – BP – 12/31/13

TABLE OF CONTENTS

Chapter One

Picky Eater

"Tuna salad? Yuck!"

"Lucas, you're a picky eater," Dad laughs. He makes my lunch for school. But I don't always like what he puts in my lunch box.

TUNA

MAYO

Wheat

Today we're going to the supermarket.
I'll pick out food for tomorrow's lunch.

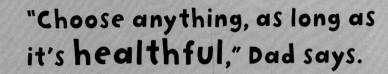

"Choose anything, as long as it's **healthful**," Dad says.

LOCALLY GROWN

Food is made of nutrients. Our bodies use nutrients to stay healthy. Vitamins and minerals are nutrients. So are proteins, carbohydrates, and fats.

Dad says eating well keeps us healthy.
Good food gives our bodies energy.

Energy is the power to move or grow.

It helps us learn and play.

Your body needs water too. It keeps your muscles and mind working right. Did you know you can get water from food? Just bite into a juicy fruit or vegetable.

Chapter Two

Five Food Groups

"We'll look for the **five food groups**," Dad says.

I pick turkey from the protein group. This group helps build strong bones and muscles. The dairy group keeps bones strong too. **Cheese, please!**

Each group includes many foods. Meat, beans, eggs, and nuts are all part of the protein group. Milk and yogurt are in the dairy group.

Popcorn is my favorite snack. It's part of the grain group. Some grains make oatmeal and pasta. Other grains go into breads and breakfast cereals.

Dad gets spinach from the vegetable group. Peas, carrots, and tomatoes are also vegetables. So are kale and celery.

A grain is the seed of a plant. Whole grain foods use all the seed. They can help keep our hearts healthy.

Now for something sweet. Cookies!

"Sugary foods taste good," Dad says. "But eating them takes our energy away. Raisins make a healthier treat. They're from the fruit group. And they're full of energy."

The fruit group has lots of sweet treats. Have berries or a melon. Eat an apple or an orange.

Chapter Three

Energy Lunch

"I need a snack," I tell Dad. I'm so hungry, I could even eat tuna salad!

"First, let's make your school lunch," Dad says. He washes the spinach. I get slices of turkey and cheese. We roll up everything in a whole grain tortilla.

The US government has tips for planning healthy meals. The plan is called MyPlate. Protein and grains make up half the meal. Fruit and vegetables make up the other half. A cup of low-fat milk goes on the side.

Whole Wheat TILLAS

For dessert, we make a **crunchy** treat.

I put popcorn and raisins in a bag.
Dad adds almonds for extra CrUnch.

Breakfast is also a big-deal meal. It wakes up your mind and body. Energy from breakfast food helps you learn better. It gives you playing power too.

There's some popcorn left over.
But not for long!

ALMONDS

Do you choose good food?
Peel an orange. Munch on carrots.
And eat healthy!

Make an Energy Lunch

Want energy for your school day? Make an energy lunch!

You'll need ingredients from the five food groups.

1) Choose something from the **protein** group. The protein group includes beans, meat, nuts, and more.

2) Choose something from the **dairy** group. The dairy group includes milk, cheese, and more.

3) Choose something from the **grain** group. The grain group includes bread, crackers, rice, and more.

4) Choose something from the **vegetable** group. The vegetable group includes avocados, carrots, broccoli, and more.

5) Choose something from the **fruit** group. The fruit group includes apples, bananas, oranges, and more.

6) Start making your lunch. You can mix the ingredients into soup or chili. Or add them to a sandwich. Don't forget dessert! Blended fruit makes a sweet smoothie.

carbohydrates: nutrients in foods such as bread and rice

energy: the ability to do work, such as moving, playing, and growing

fats: nutrients that the body uses for energy. Fats come from animals and some plants.

grain: the seed of a cereal plant. Oats, rice, and wheat are grains.

minerals: nutrients that are part of the earth. Minerals are not animals or plants.

nutrients: substances in food that the body uses to stay healthy

protein: nutrients that come from living things. Meat, eggs, and beans have protein.

vitamins: nutrients found in food

BOOKS

Cleary, Brian P. *Food Is CATegorical* series. Minneapolis: Millbrook Press, 2014.
Learn more about food with fun rhymes and cartoon cats!

Dilkes, D. H. *Vegetables.* Berkeley Heights, NJ: Enslow Elementary, 2012.
Photos in this book show how veggies are used for meals and snacks.

Hoffmann, Sara E. *Popcorn.* Minneapolis: LernerClassroom, 2014.
Check out this book to learn more about Lucas's favorite grain.

WEBSITES

Choose MyPlate
http://www.choosemyplate.gov/children-over-five.html
Visit this site to make healthy food choices, find fun recipes, and fuel up your MyPlate spaceship in the Blast Off game.

Food Champs
http://www.foodchamps.org
Play fun food games with this site's Fruit & Veggie Color Champions. Print activity sheets and coloring pages too.

PBS Kids Go!
http://pbskids.org/arthur/games/supermarket/supermarket.html
Arthur's sister D.W. is on a supermarket adventure. Help her pick the right foods for her shopping cart.

LERNER *e* SOURCE™
Expand learning beyond the printed book. Download free, complementary educational resources for this book from our website, www.lernersource.com.